# Connections

# Connections

## FINDING OUT ABOUT THE ENVIRONMENT

 Panda Books

Toronto, Canada

General Paperbacks Panda edition

ISBN 0-7736-7356-3

Illustrations: Neil McInnes
Design: David Montle
Cover photograph of David Suzuki by James Murray

THIS PROJECT WAS MADE POSSIBLE IN PART WITH A GRANT FROM
GOVERNMENT OF CANADA: SCIENCE CULTURE CANADA PROGRAM

Printed in Canada on recycled paper

Printed on paper
containing over 50%
recycled paper including
5% post-consumer fibre.

CASSETTE TAPE
Narration: David Suzuki
Executive Producers: David Suzuki, Denise Duncan
Songs composed by: Bill Iveniuk, Denise Duncan
Music Producer/Arranger: Bill Iveniuk
Vocalists: Rich Dodson, Shirley Eikhard, Bill Iveniuk, Blair and Gary Maclean, Julie Masi, Graham Shaw
Musicians: Memo Acevedo, Rich Dodson, Bill Iveniuk, Mike Konn, Carl Otway, Dave Parasz, Graham Shaw
Recorded by: Rich Dodson at Marigold Studios, Toronto
Narration recorded at: Spence-Thomas Productions, Toronto

All songs published by Upmeads Music Ltd. – PROCAN/BMI

# Contents

## VOCALISTS

Rich Dodson
"The Turpentine Story"

Shirley Eikhard
"Monarch Butterfly"
"We All Belong to the Earth"

Graham Shaw
"Just a Leaf"

Bill Iveniuk
"A Walk in the Rain Forest"
"Earthworm"
"Leave the Car at Home"
"The Three R's"

Julie Masi
"The Watercycle Polka"
"Plant a Tree"

## MUSICIANS

Memo Acevedo, Rich Dobson, Bill Iveniuk, Mike Konn, Carl Otway, Dave Parasz, Graham Shaw

All songs written by Bill Iveniuk and Denise Duncan

The first "lesson" I remember from school was the *water cycle*. Remember? Water in the oceans evaporates, forms clouds, rains on the land, runs into rivers and lakes, evaporates and goes around again. Water cartwheels around the planet. And since each of us is more than 70 per cent water, we are all made up of water that was once part of the Amazon jungle, all the oceans and the plains of Africa. We are *connected* to the whole planet and all living things through air, water and food that we all share. It's an amazing idea and teaches us that planet Earth is our home and all animals and plants in the world are our companions.

What better way is there to celebrate this beautiful world than by song? Join us as we explore our connections.

— David Suzuki

Activity Book

# RAIN FORESTS

DID YOU KNOW: There are over 50,000 known types of tree in the rain forest along the Amazon River in South America.

# A Walk in the Rain Forest

Hey, what was that?
Was that a bird?

In the rain forest, you'll see butterflies
Yeah, they're as big as a bird
There's nothing wrong with your eyes
You'll see a butterfly as big as a bird
In a rain forest.

Something's moving over there. ... What is it?

Was it a frog jumping up on a log?
Or was it that old lizard? He 's as big as a dog
Oh yeah, we'll see so many creatures
Even when we stop to rest
In this rain forest.

CHORUS: And at the top of the trees
        You'll see those busy little monkeys
        As they're hanging and they're swinging from the vines
        Under a canopy of leaves
        Fleeting shadows startle you
        We're in for a mysterious time.

Look out for the snake. ... Just kidding.

There's lots of snakes
Sometimes they live on the ground
Sometimes they climb in the trees
And if we don't make a sound
We can get a little closer
To the ones hanging down
In a rain forest.

We'll watch the spiders
Making amazing webs
And then we'll see a flash of colours
Flying over our heads
It's just canaries and parrots
Going back to their nests
In a rain forest.

CHORUS: And at the top of the trees
You'll see those busy little monkeys
As they're hanging and they're swinging from the vines
Under a canopy of leaves
Fleeting shadows startle you
We're in for a mysterious time
We're in for a mysterious time.

Walking in a rain forest with you
I'd like to be walking in a rain forest with you
Walking in a rain forest with you.

"Hello. I'm David Suzuki. A few months ago, I visited the tropical rain forest along the Amazon River in South America. It was unbelievably beautiful as brightly coloured birds and butterflies flitted through the shadows. And everywhere it was green, with plants of every imaginable shape. Long vines, giant ferns, huge trees. Of course, trees are not just nice to look at. Where do oranges, peaches and nuts come from? Trees! What is used to make paper? Trees! Trees do something else, too. They are like the lungs of the planet. Let me explain. Take a deep breath. The gas your body takes in to keep it healthy is oxygen. Now breathe out. The gas you breathe out contains a waste, carbon dioxide. Trees take that carbon dioxide and give out oxygen in exchange. And all of the air cleaned by trees circulates around the world. The air in Canada was once in Brazil, Africa and Russia."

# Word Find

Many of the plants we eat are the "cousins" of plants that grow in tropical rain forests. Find some on these plants in the puzzle.

| D | R | O | B | A | N | A | N | A |
|---|---|---|---|---|---|---|---|---|
| E | S | O | R | A | N | G | E | W |
| R | I | C | E | K | I | W | I | R |
| B | C | A | S | H | E | W | E | S |
| P | I | N | E | A | P | P | L | E |
| E | A | S | C | O | F | F | E | E |

Answers: banana, orange, pineapple, cashew, rice, kiwi, coffee

# LEAVES

# Just a Leaf

Don't tell me
It's just a leaf ... oh, no
Don't you tell me that

When you're walking down a street
Take a look at a tree
Well, I bet you didn't know it's a factory
So why don't you take a closer look and see
Let's start with the roots growing in the ground
They take a little bit of water from the earth around
To every single leaf that's in that tree
That's right ... that's what the roots do.

Chorus: Ooo, don't say it's just a leaf, just a leaf
         Ooo, don't tell me it's just a leaf, just a leaf.

A little daylight here, a little water there
The little air you breathe out, they all do their share
In that simple-looking leaf you're holding there.

Well, a leaf makes food to help the tree grow
It makes sugar glucose, and don't you know
That it's making oxygen for you and me.

Chorus: Ooo, don't say it's just a leaf, just a leaf
         Ooo, don't tell me it's just a leaf, just a leaf.

That's right, it's a leaf factory
And it's making oxygen
Right in your own backyard.

Chorus: Ooo, don't say it's just a leaf, just a leaf
       Ooo, don't tell me it's just a leaf, just a leaf.

When you're walking down a street
Take a look at a tree
Well, I bet you didn't know it's a factory
So why don't you take a closer look and see.

Daylight comes here every day
And it gives the leaf life to pass your way
I said, the daylight comes here every day
And it gives the leaf life to pass your way …

So, don't tell me it's just a leaf, oh no
Don't tell me it's just a leaf.

"In order to grow and produce the oxygen we need, plants must have water. In fact, all living things need water. Three-quarters of the planet Earth is covered with salty water in oceans and seas. Animals and plants that live on land can't drink salty water. It makes them sick. There is also water in lakes and rivers and deep underground. This is 'sweet' water — fresh water that comes from rain. So where does the rain come from? The sky, of course. But how does the water get up there?"

# Leaf rubbings

You will need:

Thin paper

Crayons with the paper label taken off

Large leaves

Tape

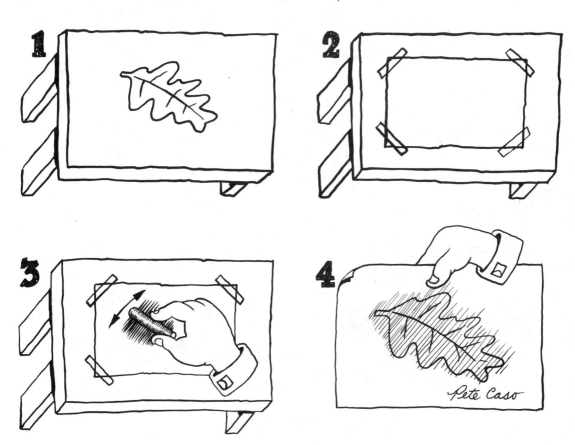

Put the leaves flat on the table. Put the paper on top of the leaves and tape the paper to the table to stop it from moving. Using the crayon lengthways, rub back and forth gently across the paper.

# WATER

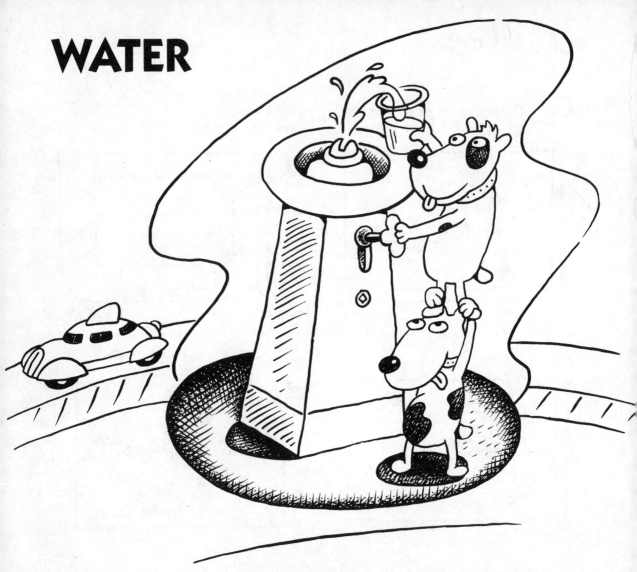

DID YOU KNOW: If all the water vapor in the air fell to Earth as rain at the same time it would cover the entire surface of the Earth with 2.5 cm (1 inch) of water.

# The Water Cycle Polka

Little drops of water, they rise up, up, up, up
And although you can't see them, they go up, up, up, up
They're rising from the oceans and the rivers and lakes
But hey, this will work out great
Because the same water vapour turns into a cloud
And when the temperature starts to fall
Those same drops of water can't stay in that cloud
They're far too heavy now to stay up at all.

Here comes that rain — it's falling, it falls down, down, down, down
It just keeps going round
Just goes up, then comes down
Yeah, the same amount of water's always been around here
It goes up, then comes down all year.
Because the same water vapour turns into a cloud
And when the temperature starts to fall
Those same drops of water can't stay in that cloud
They're far too heavy now to stay up at all
Hey, look! A rain cloud!

Here comes that rain — it's falling, it falls down, down, down, down
It just keeps going round. Just goes up, then comes down
Yeah, the same amount of water's always been around here
It goes up, then comes down all year.
Because the same water vapour turns into a cloud
And when the temperature starts to fall
Those small drops of water can't stay in that cloud
They're far too heavy now to stay up at all
Down they come! Here comes the rain!

Little drops of water, they rise up, up, up, up
And although you can't see them, they go up, up, up, up
They're rising from the oceans and the rivers and lakes
But hey, this will work out great
Because the same water vapour turns into a cloud
And when the temperature starts to fall
Those small drops of water can't stay in that cloud
They're far too heavy now to stay up at all.

Little drops of water, they rise up, up, up, up
And although you can't see them, they go up, up, up, up
They're rising from the oceans and the rivers and lakes
But hey, this will work out great
Yeah, it's raining!

"Did you know that well over half your body is made up of water? When the water levels in your body start to drop, you feel thirsty. All animals need fresh, clean water to drink if they are to stay healthy. Even tiny creatures like butterflies will perch on a leaf and sip a raindrop. Do you know what a monarch butterfly looks like? It has wings painted orange, black and white. I'm sure you've seen lots of them in your backyard or in the park. Have you noticed that as soon as you begin to feel the first cool touch of autumn, the monarch butterflies disappear? Where do they go? The amazing answer is that all the monarch butterflies from Canada and the United States east of the Rocky Mountains migrate over long distances every day for up to two months. They travel to reach a small area of a forest in Mexico. They have probably been going to the same spot for 10,000 years. Although none of the butterflies has ever made the journey before, somehow they know where to go."

# Making snowflakes

Look at some snowflakes under a magnifying glass. No two snowflakes are the same, though they all have six sides. You can make your own paper snowflakes.

You will need:

Paper
Scissors
A twisted paper clip for
   a hanger

**1** **2** **3**

**4** **5**

**6** **7**

*unfold!*

# BUTTERFLIES

DID YOU KNOW: Many birds avoid the monarch butterfly, despite its appealing color. This is because monarch butterflies contain a nasty-tasting poison that would kill the birds. This deadly poison is made when the monarch digests its main food – milkweed.

# Monarch Butterfly

Monarch butterfly . . .

Chorus: How do they find the strength to fly so far?
        It must be a miracle
        How do they know the way, do they follow a star?
        It must be a miracle, it must be a miracle.

When the summer days go by
There'll be thousands of them in the sky
So say goodbye for now
As they go gliding and flying
Like magical feathers
Day after day. It should go on forever
Monarch butterfly.

At the end of a winter's sleep
In a Mexican forest
You'll soon see a miracle
The warm sun dries their wings in that Mexican forest
It's part of the miracle, part of the miracle.

As they catch the northbound winds
Once again their life cycle begins
And with the summer breeze
You'll see those magical flyers
Go higher and higher and higher and higher and higher and higher
It must be a miracle.

Chorus: How do they find the strength to fly so far?
　　　　It must be a miracle
　　　　How do they know the way? Do they follow a star?
　　　　It must be a miracle, it must be a miracle.

Yeah, they catch the northbound winds
And once again their life cycle begins
And with the summer breeze
You'll see those magical flyers
Go higher and higher and higher and higher.

Chorus: How do they find the strength to fly so far?
　　　　It must be a miracle
　　　　How do they know the way? Do they follow the stars?
　　　　It must be a miracle.

"One of the favourite foods of the monarch butterfly is a plant called milkweed. All animal life on the entire planet Earth depends either directly or indirectly on plants. And plants get their food from the soil through their roots. So all living things, plants and animals, depend on the life developed from the Earth. Many call it Mother Earth because, like mothers, it gives birth to new life. Next time you go outside, pick up a handful of dirt and look at it closely. You'll find pebbles, dead leaves, insects, seeds, roots and maybe, if you're lucky, something long and slippery and very wiggly. ..."

# Color a monarch butterfly

Color the shaded parts of the drawing orange.

# EARTHWORMS

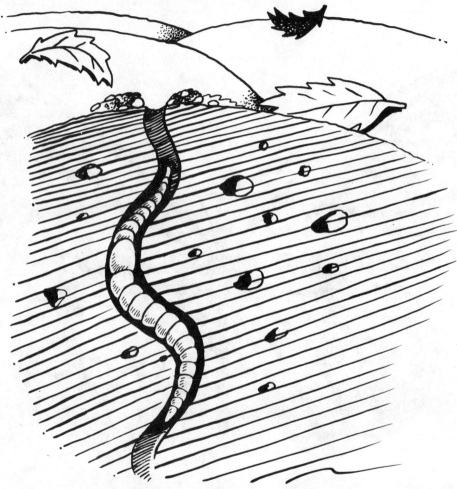

DID YOU KNOW: If you rub your finger very gently along the sides of an earthworm you will feel little bristles, called *setae*. These bristles stick in the earth and make it harder for birds to pull the earthworms out of their burrows.

# Earthworm

Wiggly, squiggly, jiggly doo
Be careful with your shovel, or you'll cut him in two
He's your backyard buddy and he lives in the ground
He's long and slimy and he's always around.

He doesn't eat bones and he doesn't eat cake
And he doesn't have a nickel for a chocolate shake
He likes to eat dead leaves
He likes to take it out of sight
He takes them in his tunnel
That's his dinner tonight.

Chorus: 'Cause he's an earthworm, earthworm
         He's living in your backyard
         Earthworm, earthworm ...

He doesn't have ears, and he doesn't have eyes
He doesn't have lungs, and he never cries
He's a simple little creature
Doesn't even have a nose
He won't be sneezing on your little toes
But there's a couple of jobs that he likes to do
He makes rich new soil from those leaves he chews
And the other little job that keeps him busy for a while
Is mixing up the soil with a wiggle and a smile.

Chorus: 'Cause he's an earthworm, earthworm
He's working in your backyard
Earthworm, earthworm . . .

He's just a sensitive fellow
He likes to eat dead leaves
He doesn't want to go fishing
There's nothing up his sleeve, no, no.

And so the next time that you see a little worm outside
He'll be eating dead leaves
He's never satisfied
Yeah, he eats them and he wiggles all over the place
He's your backyard buddy with the wormy face.

Wiggly, squiggly, jiggly doo
Be careful with your shovel, or you'll cut him in two.
He's your backyard buddy and he lives in the ground
He's long and slimy and he's always around.

Chorus: 'Cause he's an earthworm, earthworm
He's living in your backyard
Earthworm, earthworm . . .

He's just a sensitive fellow
He likes to eat dead leaves
He doesn't want to go fishing.
There's nothing up his sleeve ... earthworm.

Ch- ch- chewing on dead leaves
Earthworm
He's making rich new topsoil
Earthworm
He does not want to go fishing
Earthworm
He's your backyard buddy
Earthworm ...

"Air, water and soil are not made out of nothing. There's only so much of it, so it has to be used over and over. We call it recycling. Nature is a wonderful recycler. Earthworms recycle dead leaves and turn them into new, rich soil. Trees take carbon dioxide and exchange it for oxygen. Carbon dioxide in the air traps heat from the sun. Too much carbon dioxide makes the weather hot and dry, so farmers can't grow enough food for all the people who live on the Earth. Trees help keep our planet healthy. Rain forests are particularly important. They give off 'sweet' water that falls to Earth as rain, and they help cool the Earth by removing carbon dioxide from the air … and yet these rain forests are being cut down at a tremendous rate."

# How to make a wormery

You will need:
A large wide-mouthed glass jar
An old piece of nylon stocking
An elastic
Damp soil
Sand
2 or 3 earthworms

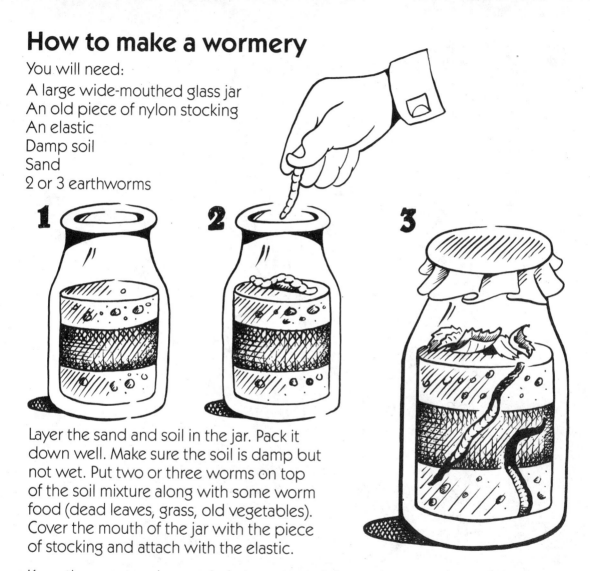

Layer the sand and soil in the jar. Pack it down well. Make sure the soil is damp but not wet. Put two or three worms on top of the soil mixture along with some worm food (dead leaves, grass, old vegetables). Cover the mouth of the jar with the piece of stocking and attach with the elastic.

Keep the wormery in a cool, dark cupboard. Spray the top of the wormery with water every day. Every second day add small bits of worm food. When you get tired of taking care of your earthworms, please let them go where you found them.

# PLANTS

DID YOU KNOW: In one year a family can, with no effort, throw away the equivalent of six trees' worth of paper. So if you live on a street of 50 houses, the people on your street throw out the equivalent of 300 trees' worth of paper a year.

# Plant a Tree

We're all packed up, we've got our lunch
We're heading out of town in one big bunch
Oh, we're going to plant some trees
I'll tell you, you'll tell me
We'll both tell someone else, that makes three
Oh, we're going to plant some trees.

Chorus: So won't you come along and plant a tree
We'll plant them everywhere universally
We'll plant them in the cities and the country
We all can help to make amends
We're all in this together, my friend.

I had a dream — I hope it comes true
People everywhere had an apple to chew
Oh, we're going to plant some trees
A tree in the wind is my favourite sight
It's cleaning the air, yes, it's making it right
Oh, we're going to plant some trees.

Chorus: So won't you come along and plant a tree
We'll plant them everywhere universally
We'll plant them in the cities and the country
We all can help to make amends
We're all in this together, my friend.

So come on, let's go, we've got a job to do
'Cause they're cutting down trees as I'm talking to you
Oh, we're going to plant some trees
We're all packed up, we've got our lunch
We're heading out of town in one big bunch
Oh, we're going to plant some trees.

Chorus: So won't you come along and plant a tree
        We'll plant them everywhere universally
        We'll plant them in the cities and the country
        We all can help to make amends
        We're all in this together, my friend.

"Many trees and plants are damaged every year by acid rain. Acid rain is just that – rainwater that is a weak acid. Smoke from factories and exhaust fumes from cars contain tiny particles of sulphur and nitrogen. These are carried up into the air where they mix with water vapour to form sulphuric acid and nitric acid. These acids eventually fall to earth as acid rain. Acid rain eats away at buildings and statues and can kill fresh fish and plants. This dirtying of the air is called 'air pollution.' What can you do about air pollution?"

# Grow some seeds

You will need:

Seeds — collect seeds from apples, peaches, oranges — anything with seeds
A bowl of water
A shallow pan

Small pebbles — enough to cover the bottom of the pan
Soil
A clear plastic bag

Soak the seeds in a bowl of water for one day. Put a layer of small pebbles on the bottom of the shallow pan. Add some soil. Sprinkle the seeds on top, and add more soil to cover them. Place the pan in the plastic bag. Tie the bag shut. Put the pan in a sunny, warm place. After about a week you should see some seedlings. As the seedlings get bigger, move them to larger pots.

# ACID RAIN

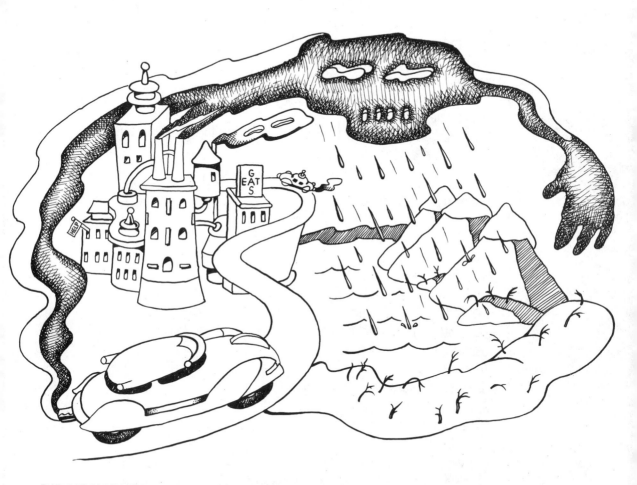

DID YOU KNOW: Acid rain has killed almost all the fish and plants in 14,000 lakes in Ontario and Eastern Canada. Another 40,000 lakes are in danger of dying.

# Leave the Car at Home

It's a hot summer night
You're going to the store
Going to the store for ice cream.
It's not very far
Should you take the car?
The answer is simple — it seems that you should
Leave the car at home
When it's not very far to go
Get a little exercise
Walk.

It's early in the morning
It's time for school
You know you don't want to be late
Get away from that TV
Slide into your shoes
Walk to the school with your mates. Why don't you
Leave the car at home?
Turn off the TV and go
Leave the car at home
Turn off the TV and
Walk to school
Run to school
Bike to school
Should you take the car?
No way!
No way, you say ... no way, no way, no way.

You're going to visit a friend
Who lives around the block
It's cold and it's snowing outside
Put on your scarf and your woolly socks
Get on your sled and slide. Why don't you
Leave the car at home?
When it's not very far to go
Leave the car at home
You can dress up warm and go
For a little winter exercise.

You want to go to the corner
For something to eat
Maybe a burger and fries
Well, if you walk to the corner
That's really neat
You won't be polluting the skies
Why don't you
Leave the car at home?
Walk to the corner, don't drive
Leave the car at home
Yeah, walk to the corner, don't drive
Don't drive that car
Don't drive that car
Should you take the car? No way!
Leave the car at home!

"We all need clean air to breathe, and leaving the car at home is one way to cut down air pollution. Clean water is just as important as clean air. Many people live close to a lake. When these people turn on the taps in their homes, the water that comes out is lake water. The water is used for drinking, cooking, watering plants, bathing and for making things like electricity, paper and plastics. When the water is used, it is poured back into the lakes."

# Join the dots

Find out what is polluting the air.

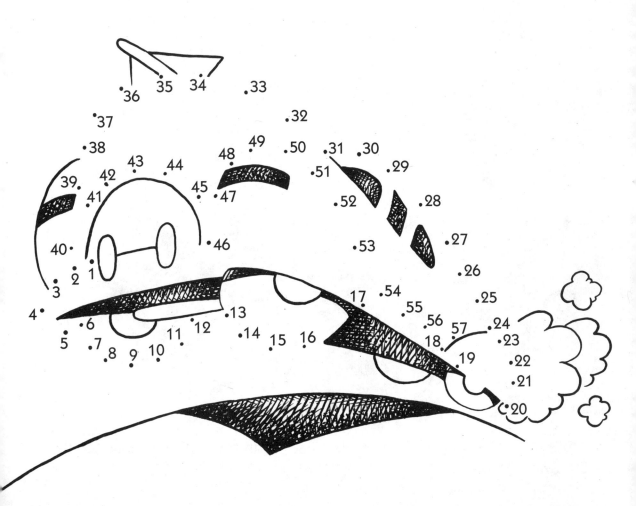

45

# WATER POLLUTION

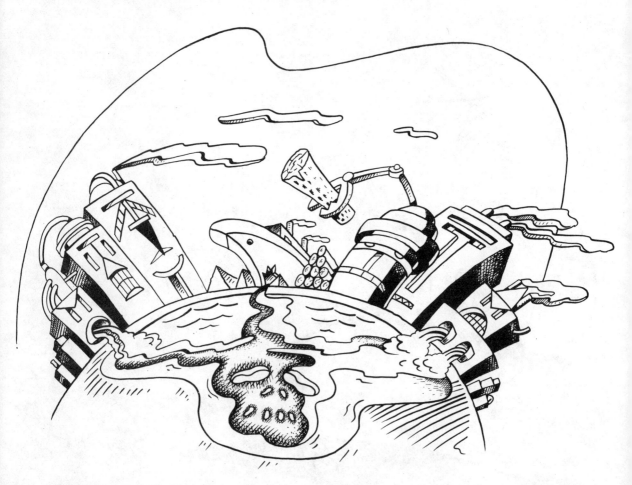

DID YOU KNOW: The beluga whales that live in the polluted mouth of the St. Lawrence River are so full of poisons that when they die they have to be treated as toxic waste.

# The Turpentine Story

Party!
I was running around at my birthday party
With my birthday cake on my chin
I was having a ball, until I hit the wall
I guess that's where my story begins
I saw stars in the sky. I was so dizzy I wanted to cry, cry, cry
That's when I bumped into Sue
She did a back flip or two
Then she flattened the dog like a dime
Then, oh, my gosh, she fell into the paint
And I'm in trouble again
Because here comes Mom, Baby Sue's in the paint
And I'm in trouble again. Oh, boy, normal day.

Out came the turpentine. Baby Sue was still crying
As my mom washed the paint down the drain
And then she suddenly stopped
She gave me that look
And I was sure I was in for some pain
She said, "Hey, birthday boy
I just made a gargantuan mistake." Gargantuan?
"I remembered a book I was reading last night
And it talked about poisoning lakes
Oh, my gosh, I just put turpentine and paint down the drain
Oh, my gosh, I just poisoned the lake
I'll never do that again." I sure hope not.

Well, then she picked up my sister. She settled her down
Then she told me to go get that book
She said, "Pollution's a problem that we all have to face
Yes, we all have to change our outlook"
I said, "Here I go, Mom"
As I flew down the hall like a jet. "Look out!"
I took the corner too fast
I started to laugh
Then I flattened the dog like a dime
Oh, my gosh. I fell into the paint
And I'm in trouble again.
Because here comes Mom, I'm all covered in paint
And I'm in trouble again. That's my story.

And now we won't put turpentine and paint down the drain.
No, no. We will not be poisoning the lake
'Cause what we put into the water
Will come back again.
That would be such a silly mistake.

We won't put turpentine and paint down the drain.
No, no. We will not be poisoning the lake
'Cause what we put into the water
Will come back again.
That would be such a silly mistake.
Don't put poisonous waste down the drain … no!

"Pollution is a very serious problem, but there are lots of little things every one of us can do to help fight pollution. For example, we can cut down on the amount of garbage we produce. When the garbage is collected from outside your home, it is taken to a dump or it is burned. Either way it can give off dangerous gases and allow poisons to get into the water in the ground. And all that garbage takes a great deal of precious space. So you can help to save space and cut down on pollution by reducing the amount of garbage at home. Don't buy toys just because of fancy packaging. Reuse things like the plastic bags that go into your lunch box and recycle pop cans and bottles."

# Make a pond terrarium

You will need:

A large glass jar — you may be able to get a large empty mayonnaise jar from a restaurant

Aquarium gravel from a pet store or sand Do not use beach sand; it is too fine

Pond water

Plastic bags and pails for collecting specimens

Food for your specimens — a pet store or library should be able to provide the information

An outing to a pond or marsh

Fill the bottom of the jar with aquarium gravel or sand. If you use sand, be sure to rinse it clean. Allow the sand to settle before adding animals. Now you are ready to collect your specimens. Look for snails, crayfish, water insects, tadpoles and newts. Be sure to get some pond plants and any food your specimens need.

When you are tired of taking care of your pond terrarium, please empty it back into the pond where you collected your specimens.

# GARBAGE

DID YOU KNOW: The plastic that you put in your household garbage that goes to the dump takes between 200 and 300 years to decompose (rot). Plants and vegetables in a compost heap rot in a couple of months.

# The Three R's

There's garbage in the rivers
There's garbage in the sea
There's garbage everywhere I look
It's really bugging me.
There's garbage in the farmyards
There's garbage at the zoo
We're making too much garbage
But here's one thing you can do.
Learn some ways to reduce
Learn to reduce . . . all that garbage.

Hey, those plastic baby diapers
We could stack them to the moon.
And those garbage dumps are getting full
Of plastic plates and spoons.
We can't get rid of all that junk,
It just won't disappear.
We've got to think of what we're doing,
Think until it's clear.
We've got to learn some ways to reuse,
Learn to reuse all that garbage.

And don't put all that garbage out beside the street
No, no.
Turn some of that garbage into compost heaps
Yes, yes.
There's way too much garbage and I'm feeling trapped
So don't buy vegetables and fruits in plastic wrap.
Learn some ways to reduce . . . all that garbage,
Learn to reduce . . .

Those old newspapers in the corner like a lump
They're not ordinary garbage, so don't send them to the dump.
'Cause when you recycle paper you'll be saving lots of trees
You'll be helping Mother Nature. Yeah, she'll really be so pleased.
And that's a nice thing to do ... that's very nice.

There's garbage in the mountains
There's garbage out in space
There's garbage everywhere you look
It's really a disgrace.
But there's lots of things that you can do to win the garbage game.
You could start by telling everyone to start to use their brain.
They should learn some ways to reduce.
Learn to reduce ... all that garbage.

And don't put all that garbage out beside the street,
Turn some of that garbage into compost heaps.
There's way too much garbage and I'm feeling trapped
So don't buy vegetables and fruits in plastic wrap.
Learn some ways to reduce ... all that garbage.
Learn some ways to reuse ... that garbage.
Learn to recycle ... garbage.

"The Earth is a magical place. It is the magic of gently falling snow, butterflies and spring flowers. It's our home, and all living things on the entire planet Earth are connected, because we share the same air, water and even earth through the foods we eat. If we hurt our surroundings, everyone is hurt. We all have to be responsible and do our best to make this a cleaner, healthier planet to live on, because it's our Mother Earth."

# Maze

Find the path to take the bottles and cans to the recycling box, the paint cans to the toxic waste dump and the fruit and vegetable peels and egg shells to the compost heap.

# THE EARTH

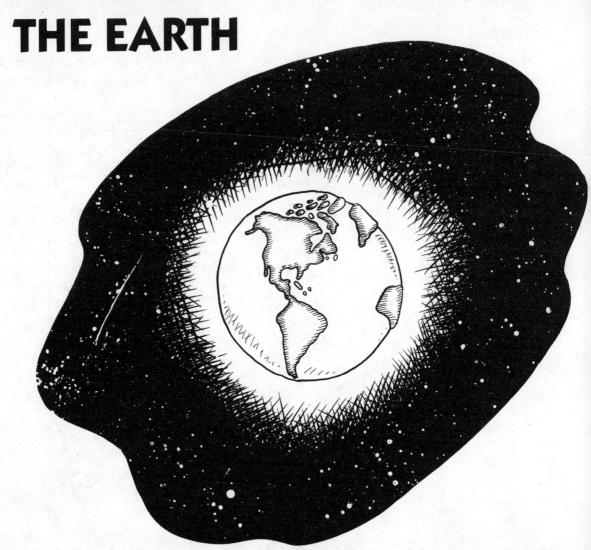

DID YOU KNOW: Scientists think that the Earth was formed about 4,600 million years ago from a spinning cloud of dust and gases.

# We all Belong to the Earth

We all belong to the Earth
This planet is our home.
We all belong to the Earth
It is our home.

We all belong to the Earth
We live in a beautiful place.
We all belong to the Earth
Alone in space.

We all belong to the Earth
Every animal, flower and tree.
We all belong to the Earth
It's you and me.

We all belong to the Earth
We all need clean water and air.
We all belong to the Earth
It's for all to share.

We all belong to the Earth
This planet is our home.
We all belong to the Earth
It is our home.

We all belong to the Earth
We live in a beautiful place.
We all belong to the Earth
Alone in space.

We all belong to the Earth
Every animal, flower and tree.
We all belong to the Earth
It's you and me.

We all belong to the Earth
We all need clean water and air.
We all belong to the Earth
It's for all to share.

# Close-up photos

Here are six close-up photos of plants and animals you could find close to your home. Do you know what they are?

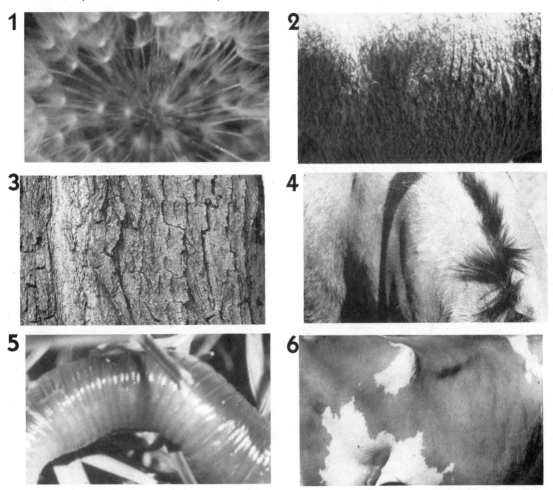

**1** **2** **3** **4** **5** **6**